Witches

To grannies the world over

First published by Granada Publishing 1981

Text © Granada Publishing 1981
Illustrations © Colin Hawkins 1981

Adapted and published in the United States
in 1985 by Silver Burdett Company, Morristown, New Jersey

ISBN 0-382-09132-9
Library of Congress Catalog Card No. 85-40425

Printed in Italy by New Interlitho, Milan

Witches

by
Colin Hawkins and
an old witch

Silver Burdett Company
Morristown, New Jersey

Pointed hat ~

Rare Black Ferret
very powerful
talisman against
pick pockets.

Raven

Long black gown

foraging stroller.

Which is Witch?

According to ancient writings,

"A witch be known by her great age, wrinkled face, furrowed brow, hairy lip, fanged teeth, squint eye, squeaking voice, scolding tongue, ragged coat and the cat or dog by her side."

This is, of course, a very good description of lots of people, especially grannies, and even more especially of old grannies. Even if your granny has all these qualities, it still doesn't mean that she is a witch. Watch for other signs. Ask yourself these questions:

1 Has your granny a fondness for wearing long black gowns and tall pointed hats?
2 Does she cook weeds, roots and herbs in enormous black pots?
3 Does your granny like to dance around the garden at midnight? If so, does she dance a) alone, b) with her cronies, c) only at full moon, d) at other times?
4 Can your granny raise storms at sea, call up the wind, bring rain?
5 Does your granny fly? If so, does she fly a) on her broomstick, b) on the back of her cat, c) on an airplane?
6 Can your granny change her shape? Have you ever seen her as a) a butterfly, b) a raven, c) a spider?
7 Can your granny cure a) fevers, b) chills, c) bad moods?

If you answered yes to any of these questions, your granny is almost certainly a witch. If you answered no to them all, here is one further test you can apply:

Ask your granny if she likes tea. A true witch will answer yes.

If you decide that your granny is definitely a witch, read this book and find out more about the powers and practices of her kind. And be kind to her, witches need a lot of love.

Familiar atop a familiar

Very wise familiar

A familiar hat

A furry familiar

A familiar smile

Suspended familiar

A familiar pair

Spotted familiar

Looks Familiar

If you are talking behind your granny's back, make sure her cat is not listening. For her cat is probably not a real cat at all. It is probably her familiar, an imp that has taken the form of a cat. Familiars are used by witches to gather information and gossip. They take messages to other witches. They help to gather ingredients for spells and generally make themselves useful.

Not all familiars are cats, of course. They can be dogs, birds, toads, alligators and even spiders, but cats are most popular because they can forecast the weather and help a witch to change it. Watch your granny's cat. If it claws at the carpet or at the curtains, it is raising the wind. If it washes its ears or sneezes, rain will come.

Though familiars are a great help to a witch and good company, they often become too familiar. Cats will often walk all over their witch. The expression "familiarity breeds contempt" comes from this habit.

"Watch the birdie".

An over familiar familiar.

Weather cocks are a protection against the powers of darkness.

Beware of bats in the hair.

13

To be near an elder tree or witch oak after dusk is to run the risk of being placed in the power of witches.

Broomstick shed.

Beware of cats that stare.

Home Sour Home

Witches tend to live in houses of great age, but it is not always easy to tell a witch's house for certain. Signs to look for are: an unlucky number on the door; a very slender garage; multiple cat flaps; blackened windows; a weather vane blowing backwards; a witch answering the door. If you suspect that a house belongs to a witch (unless it is your granny's) do not go too close. You could become bewitched.

Inside, the witch's house is well furnished, with molted cat-fur carpets, raven flock wallpaper and cobweb curtains at the windows. Upstairs, the bedrooms contain beds, baskets, bees' nests, perches, alligator cots and cats' cradles.

Witches are often called out at night to cast spells or perform a bit of hocus pocus, so they have to snatch what sleep they can, snoozing in an easy chair or dozing in front of the television. Some people believe that witches never sleep at all. Ask your granny if she sleeps well.

You will notice that witches never have newspapers delivered to their homes. Stale news is of no interest to them. They prefer to read the future in the flames of the fire. Books are another matter. A witch needs a good library of recipe books and spellbooks, and notebooks for writing up new spells. Not only bookworms will be found in the library but book caterpillars, book beetles and book spiders – even the odd bookfrog will slide along the shelves.

Bats hate water

Baths are rarely if ever a private affair.

Soap wort lather.

A familiar cat scrubbing a familiar back.

Hubble Bubble Bath

Contrary to popular belief, witches like to wash or bath every day, and most wash and curl their hair at least once a week. Bubbles are a must. Soapwort leaves, bruised, tied in muslin, and agitated with water produce a luxurious foam in minutes. To create an especially soothing bath after a hectic night, many witches add lavender to the water, a favorite witch scent. See if your granny likes lavender.

Bathtime is also beauty time, with extra care given to hair and complexion. Secret health and beauty recipes are handed down from witch mother to witch daughter. Ointments, herbs, lotions, shampoos, powders and scents, all combine to give the characteristically sleek shiny locks and soft downy skin of a young witch. Lips are polished and fangs varnished.

The problem of over familiar familiars often becomes acute at bathtime.

Bath water thrown over leeks will encourage hardy growth.

The normal height of a witch is between 5 and 9 feet (including hat.)

Night Light Hat. complete with funnel and snuffer, used for reading in bed, and on moonless nights

Hat brim can be folded down and tied over the ears in cold weather.

Open finger mittens

Black vest

Portable cauldron

Secret pockets

Liberty Bodice

Winter warmth bloomers.

Black stretch stockings

Stout leather boots

Witch Wear

Witches are old fashioned in their choice of clothes. They believe that their garments should be hard wearing and good value for money. Clothes should be warm for chilly October flights and reasonably waterproof, especially during June rain bottling. They need to be of a color that will not show cauldron splashes or garden grubbings.

Most important, clothes should be comfortable, allowing complete freedom of movement for arm waving and leg jerking spells. The classic witch gown has extra deep pockets for keeping such witch essentials as sandwiches, a thermos, safety pins, string, old stockings, toads and garters.

A Witch's Bag.
and some of its contents

Snap purse.

Pocket spell book for pocket spells.

Flying ointment.

Whistle for calling up the wind, and police dogs.

Wart pricking pin.

Small umbrella, for quick showers and squalls.

Snap Cackle Pop

A prune a day makes witches gay.

A breakfast of ant eggs eaten raw, will restore the senses.

Pains in the belly can be cured by jelly

Bat's will rarely, if ever get up in time for breakfast.

Dropping in for breakfast

Second helpings

Toasted cheese, please.

Witches eat heartily at breakfast. Most are especially fond of witch's grits, made from preserved frogspawn. A favorite second course is dawn-gathered toadstools on toast. After that, for the sour toothed, there is delicious sloe jam, with acorn bread and steaming hot dandelion coffee. In the old days, witches had to cast a spell to sour their milk, but nowadays sour cream can easily be had from the supermarket.

Not so with food for the familiars; very few stores stock canned toad food, raven seed, batburgers or choice cuts for alligators. So breakfast can take a long time, even with an imaginative witch at the stove. And with so many to feed it's not surprising that the cupboard is soon bare.

A cat on the mat is a cat that is fat.

...And when the cupboard is bare...

The spell to make the bus come.

Note use of thumb.

Shock in Store

Sometimes this spell can be too strong.

Whistling up sausages.

Ninety per cent of butchers say that they can recognize a witch in their shop.

Only the stalest bread will do for a really fussy witch.

French bread should be wrapped before leaving the bakery.

Year candle.

Candle stick maker →

Since the invention of electricity, witches have been more welcome at the candlestickmakers.

In times gone by, a witch had to go from store to store for her provisions. Today she can shop in half the time and with twice the fun. The supermarket has become a great center for witches meeting, exchanging news, gossip and the latest spells, and taking part in the weekly race to the check out. It is worth noting that witches like to shop between 5:30 and 7:00pm on Friday evenings – a time to avoid supermarkets if at all possible.

Green Fingers

Few stores stock the variety of ingredients that a witch needs constantly at hand for her spells. So a witch must cultivate her garden, keeping the ground free from flowers that choke the weeds, and clearing mushrooms from space where nettles and toadstools could grow.

Because witches can hear a plant in pain, they are careful to cast plant sleeping spells before cutting a single stem. No crying creepers, shrieking violets, mournful moss or wisteria with hysteria will be found in a witch's garden. Nor will you find plants tied to stakes or forced to stand in rows against the wall.

Favorite witch plants are nettles, dandelions, the tastier toadstools, ground elder, chickweed, rosemary, foxgloves, cucumbers and roses. See if your granny has any of these plants in her garden.

Hollyhocks: a good remedy for spongy gums.

Cucumbers, pumpkins, watercress and claws Will soothe a rose that is covered in sores

A welcome crow

To stay in fine
fettle, eat a
nettle

Dandelions
Will induce restful
sleep rarely.

Chickweed
A cure for itch
and scabs.

Not much room
for mushrooms

One or two drops of bats blood, mixed with deadly night shade, foxglove and the grease of a boar, make an excellent flying ointment.

It is thought that there are more witch cures for warts than there are warts in the world.

'A moth in the broth will cure your cough'.

'Toe nails, that are grown long are useful to bind a spell strong.

Spelling Lessons

Throughout the centuries people have feared witches. In a flash, one of these old crones might transform you into a cat or a toadstool or a bat, or even, if you are a prince, into a frog. Now, there is no doubt that some witches have a nastier side to their magic, a little bit of mischief here, a little bit of hocum there. But, on the whole, witches have usually practiced their arts to good purpose. Worn out by the toil and trouble of slaving over a hot cauldron, many witches have grown old before their time, just trying to help ordinary people.

To make an active potion, the witch needs not only the right mixture, cooked at the exact temperature, but she also needs to know the precise form of words for casting the spell.

This involves a young witch in hours of tedious practice after school. She must take cooking lessons, study recipes, learn shorthand and typing and millions of chants, calls, shrieks, mutters and incantations. Without a good grounding in spelling, a witch cannot hope for a successful career.

The simplest spells deal with the weather. To raise a storm at sea, for instance, a witch merely has to swing a cat three times around her head and then throw it into the sea, chanting,

"Screech, screech, screech and scraw,
Make the sea rage and roar."

More difficult but more worthwhile are spells for curing ailments.

Successful rainmaking witch.　　　Dry toad.

Kill or Cure

The bag and
pebbles method.

If you have warts, try these cures:
Place in a bag as many pebbles as
you have warts and leave the
bag at a crossroads. The warts
will be transferred to whoever
picks up the bag. Or, prick your
warts with a pin and stick the
pin into an ash tree, reciting:
"Ashen tree, ashen tree, pray
take away these warts from me."
If your warts do not transfer
to the tree, ask your granny
what to do.

As a cure for
tooth ache a
dead mole
should be
worn around
the neck.

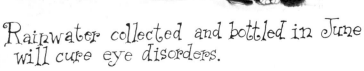

Rainwater collected and bottled in June
will cure eye disorders.

You and your family may like to try these cures and spells.

If you have a tummy ache, stand on your head for two minutes and say "Ickle, dickle, dockle day, Take this horrid pain away."

If you have a cough, stay in bed and take owl broth three times a day.

If you have a toothache, wear a dead mole around your neck.

If you have a fever, take pills of compressed spiders' webs before breakfast.

If you have sore knees, boil up some cabbage and some caterpillars with some chocolate sponge and eat the mixture at bedtime.

If you have a runny nose, hold your ears and touch your toes.

If a dog bites you, take some hair of the dog, fry it and place it on the wound together with a sprig of rosemary.

Boar's grease cures Gout
Greasy boars are not easy to find and so should be allowed to drive the bath chair occasionally

If your head aches, close your eyes, stay very still and count silently to a hundred. This cure may have to be tried over and over again before it works. And even if it doesn't work on your headache, it may cure granny's.

The cure for a dog bite

Friendship

Witches like to get together. Coffee mornings, bridge clubs,
Sunday drives, tennis tournaments and tea parties are all
good excuses for a cozy gossip. For entertainment after
a tea party the witches watch television or tell each
other's fortune in the tea leaves (witches never use
tea bags). Tea being drunk, each witch passes her cup
to the left. The witch next to her swirls it three
times in her left hand before draining off the dregs.
Patterns near the handle represent the near future,
those in the upper part more distant events and those
in the bottom the very distant future. Patterns shaped
like crosses, spades, guns, snakes, cats or toads
spell bad luck; moonshapes, clover leaves, flowers,
trees, crows and the number seven foretell good
luck. See if you can tell fortunes this way.
Ask your granny to help you at first.

After a dinner party, witches like to dance,
practicing the latest steps and listening
to the top ten, ready for the big witch
festivals. Finding suitable partners is
often a problem for witches.

A witched kettle never boils.

A slow kettle could be
bewitched and contain a toad.

A flight or cackle of Witches

Flying High

Goats can be flown if no other choice is available.

Ancient texts tell of skies black with witches flying to the Sabbath and loud with screeching and cackling. But broomstick flying is dangerous, cold and uncomfortable so most witches prefer to travel by bus, bicycle or car. In fact, they usually only fly to important witch gatherings such as Sabbaths or Halloween, or in cases of public transportation strikes or great emergency.

Witches traditionally fly on broomsticks, though sometimes they use cats, roosters, horses, large dogs or, if really desperate, goats. A horse found in the morning, tired, sweating and not fit for work might well have been hag ridden during the night. On witch Sabbaths, farmers guard their stables to keep their horses from being stolen.

Riding to the Sabbath.

Before take off, the witch must rub flying ointment all over her body.
The smell of this mixture of bat's blood, deadly nightshade, foxglove
juice and boar's grease is a sure sign that a witch will be flying tonight.

Shape changing into a bird, fly or other flying creature is a short cut
to flying. Witches can change themselves into any creature they wish,
from ants to weasels, though cats and hares are the most popular choice.
A witch is usually unable to change into a dove or a white rabbit.

Shape Shifting
Cats and hares are the
most popular form taken,
and occasionally
flies.

Shape changing
into doves was
never successful.

High Jinks

The witches' year begins at Halloween, a time when ghosts demons and children roam abroad demanding treats or offering tricks. Homes are decorated with candles in turnips and pumpkins with faces; apples are bobbed and bonfires lit.

To dance the Widdershins, (the dance of the witches) form a circle 10-15 feet in diameter around a bonfire and dance in the opposite direction to that of the sun's path around the sky.

The traditional dance around the maypole to Knees up Mother Brown.

On Halloween the witches gather at midnight and dance flush-cheeked around the flames until dawn. Round and round the bonfire, dancing widdershins, waltzing, quickstepping, slowstepping, sidestepping, twisting, shaking and just doing their thing. No other festival lives up to Halloween for fashions, flying and fun.

Some needed more purification than others.

Candlemas, for instance, is a time for cleanliness and goodliness. Witches burn candles as a sign of their purity.

On Valentine's Day, young witches place bay leaves under their pillows in order to dream of their future husbands. It is not known how accurate their dreams are.

With Bay leaves under her pillow, a girl will dream of her future husband.

May Day celebrates the start of summer and is time for more high jinks. Young witches dance around the maypole, hoping to attract enough attention to be chosen Queen of the May.

If a young witch has not found a husband by May Day, she can try again around the Midsummer's Eve bonfire.

At the harvest festival of Lammas on August 1, a girl has her last chance. Often witches bake magic cakes with the newly harvested corn to offer to their sweethearts. If they cannot charm a man with their charms, they will resort to their spells.

The first loaf of Lammas.

A coven of witches usually consists of 13 witches.

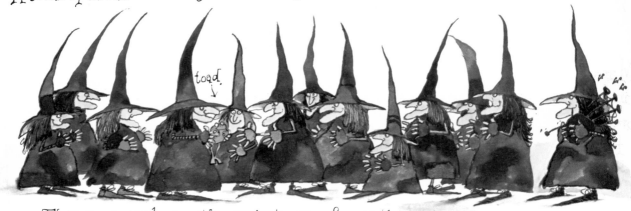

This coven is playing the ancient game of pass the toad.

Witch Facts?

A favorite spell of witches and wizards is to turn a Prince into a frog, or Rover into a toad.

If you want to know the way ask an old witch.

Witches have been known to live to a great age some well beyond 65 years.

An old witch in her later years will teach all she knows to a young novice witch.

Many witches practice great skill in the art of broomstick flying.

In ancient times both male and female witches were often said to have the ability to worry sheep.

Two worried sheep.

another worried sheep.

Misunderstood black cat

Witches are very fond of cats, especially black cats. They are the most popular choice as familiars and, like witches, have long been misunderstood.

Twins especially witch twins, have long been thought to possess unique powers. Although also regarded by many to be double trouble.

The words printed above this line are in a secret language that only witches can see. Ask your granny what they say.